ECLETUS PARROT

The Complete Beginners Guide Book On Everything You Need To Know About Ecletus Parrot Housing, Feeding, Speech And Vocalization

JAMES AUTHOR

Table of Contents

CHAPTER ONE

INTRODUCTION

Fascinating, brave and smart, eclectus parrots are captivating birds that make mind-blowing pets. Their stunning colorings, talking capacity, and loveable personalities have set up this bird as one of the maximum popular puppy parrots. This bird is one in every of the bigger parrot species, and it does require the proper proprietor with masses of time and space to residence this bird.

CHAPTER TWO

BEHAVIOR OF ECLETUS PARROT

The eclectus is a very friendly and sensible fowl species defined as gentle, tranquil, and being concerned. Eclectus parrots are also affectionate. Maximum thrive satisfactory when socialization is a part of their daily recurring. They cherish the time they spend interacting with their families. They're additionally sensitive and might quick become careworn if they experience unnoticed.

This chook will learn the ordinary and what to anticipate in your family. They experience the comings and goings, as well as being a part of it.

Around 18 months of age, the birds start to attain sexual adulthood. From time to time this brings with it a few aggressions or the instinct to "feed" anything is nearby. You may word some naughty nipping conduct. This era is referred to as bluffing, and it is exceptional to disregard it and turn to distraction strategies instead of reinforcing it. With time, they bypass thru the phase and learn what is suitable.

At the same time as each the women and men of the species make cute pets, many owners claim that males have a tendency to be a bit more trainable and agreeable. At the turn facet, women can be less depending on their owners and generally tend to deal with pressure higher. Females will also be bossier and greater aggressive than a male, particularly for the duration of breeding. Even in captivity, a woman's nesting instincts remain sturdy. You may find her looking to nest in secluded regions of your private home.

CHAPTER THREE

SPEECH AND VOCALIZATIONS OF ECLETUS PARROT

Eclectus parrots are a part of African greys as being one of the quality species for training to talk. They're quick to examine nearly anything you want to educate them. Many human beings locate them to be at the quieter facet while compared to other parrots. They have a one of a kind honk and different vocalizations that can be amusing the first few instances, but loud and startling.

Teach your bird how to speak

The first step to coaching your chicken to speak is to bond with your feathered buddy and shape reasonable expectancies of it.

Select your phrases accurately

• The fine manner to encourage your bird to speak is to pick a few short words for them to start out with. Examples of properly starter words include "hello," "bye-bye," "nite-nite," or even your hen's own name.

Simple words, while said with enthusiasm, appear to emerge as greater interesting to maximum parrots. Make certain that whilst you communicate in your chicken, you accomplish that in a satisfied, fine tone.

Watch your ecletus bird as you repeat the phrases you've got selected. If you pay close attention, you will in all likelihood see that some phrases will catch its interest more than others. Use the word that your bird responds to the most on your first "training phrase."

Repeat the word or word as frequently as viable

- The nice way to encourage birds to talk is to pick a few brief phrases for them to start off with. Examples of top starter words consist of "howdy," "bye-bye," "nite-nite," or maybe your chook's personal call.

Simple words, when said with enthusiasm, appear to come to be more exciting to maximum parrots. Make sure that whilst you speak to your fowl, you accomplish that in a satisfied, positive tone.

Watch your ecletus bird as you repeat the words you've chosen. In case you pay close interest, you will probably see that a few words will capture its interest extra than others. Use the phrase that your bird responds to the most on your first "schooling word."

Repeat the phrase or word as frequently as feasible

The quickest manner to encourage your bird to speak is to set up an education recurring and work with it every day. Even this technique, but, is not completely assured to work. While a few birds pick out up on human speech quite with ease, a few birds take months or even years to mention their first word. Some will by no means talk at all—even owners that paintings with their pets diligently every now and then emerge as with a bird that won't say a phrase.

If you feel like your bird is taking too lengthy along with his speech education, try coaching something a little bit simpler, along with whistling. Many birds find whistling much simpler than mimicking speech, and some may be extra inclined to present it a strive because of this.

With love, patience, and masses of exercise and schooling time, your bird will learn to mimic something.

Pay attention to the vocalizations that your bird makes all through the day. You will be surprised to find which you understand some of them as environmental sounds that you hear every day in your home, like phones, microwave buzzers, and doorbells.

Even in case your ecletus parrot in no way speaks a human phrase, you shouldn't experience slighted. Speech training, interaction, and socialization all help to reinforce the bond between you and your pet, so in case your bird stays silent, you could nonetheless be assured that you'll get a loveable, shrewd, and thrilling partner out of the deal—and as some distance as proudly owning a bird goes, it truly is the best part!

CHAPTER FOUR

COLOURS OF ECLETUS PARROT

Eclectus are called sexually dimorphic, meaning that you can inform the sex of the bird by means of its bodily characteristics. Male eclectus birds are an exquisite emerald inexperienced shade with vivid orange beaks and splashes of red and blue under their wings. By means of evaluation, the women are in the main vibrant purple with black beaks and deep red markings on their chests and tails. Earlier than the early twentieth century, since the male and female birds regarded so distinct, they were notion to be absolutely different species.

Eclectus feathers seem to blend. Their coloring makes for outstanding camouflage of their native habitat; you may often hear them earlier than you could see them.

Reasons for choosing an ecletus parrot as pet

Most eclectus birds can live in a multiple hen household; however a few have jealous inclinations. Make certain to give an eclectus your undivided time and interest while introducing it or any new hen or your aviary.

An eclectus lives first-rate in an aviary—eleven toes lengthy through three foot huge and seven feet excessive— mainly if you keep a pair. Those birds like to fly, climb, and stay busy. If you do now not have room for an aviary, then make sure the cage you offer is on the minimal 2 toes long via 3 toes extensive and 4 toes tall.

This species may be an amazing match for households with kids as it has a mild nature. However, they do not like to be startled and like peaceful surroundings. They're not big enthusiasts of regular loud noises like barking, crying, or screaming. Therefore, it's important to recall in case your family dynamic is a great in shape for the hen.

CHAPTER FIVE

COMMON HEALTH PROBLEMS OF ECLETUS PARROT

An eclectus is precise in that it on occasion famous toe-tapping and wing-flipping. This conduct is much like feather plucking, that's a common issue with parrots that experience unnoticed. But, when all three of those actions arise in an eclectus, it is able to be a signal of an extreme fitness difficulty. Dietary deficiencies as a result of extra nutrients and minerals (like diet A), fortified ingredients, or synthetic substances in addition to ingesting overseas gadgets like beads, or strain are possibly causes. It's essential to look an avian vet proper away.

Other health conditions that an eclectus is prone to getting encompass:

• Avian polyomavirus, a contamination that reasons pores and skin tumors

• Constricted toe syndrome, a circumstance that reasons flow to be cut off to the bird's toe

- Psittacine beak and feather disorder, a viral immune machine ailment

CHAPTER SIX

FOODS TO FEED AND NOT TO FEED YOUR ECLETUS PARROT

Foods to feed your ecletus parrot

Inside the wild, these birds opt for pomegranate, papaya, and figs, though they'll also eat plants, buds on bushes, and a few seeds. When kept as a pet, their eating regimen should encompass clean fruits, greens, and carbohydrates. Cooked pasta or grain bake—a homemade casserole just for birds—will ensure they get all the important carbohydrates.

The eclectus has a specialized digestive tract this is extraordinary from many different chicken species. This bird wishes to be fed a weight-reduction plan high in fiber and low in fats. It is also high-quality to avoid too many diet and mineral dietary supplements, which could result in digestive tumors or ordinary behavior.

Foods to avoid when feeding your ecletus parrot

Keep away from feeding parrot mixes that contain synthetic dyes, flavorings, or preservatives. Those additives could purpose your puppy to lose its stunning coloration and might also be poisonous for this touchy species.

An eclectus each day meal have to be about 8 percentage fruits and greens—the rest may be parrot pellets. Supply seeds and nuts as occasional treats. Feed this chicken twice an afternoon, as soon as upon rising, and 1 to 2 hours earlier than bedtime. Provide 1 cup of end result and vegetables and 1/3 cup of parrot blend at every feeding.

THE END